Also by MARY O'MALLEY
from Carcanet Press

Valparaiso
2012

A Perfect V
2006

The Boning Hall
2002

Playing the Octopus

MARY O'MALLEY

CARCANET

for Steve

First published in Great Britain in 2016 by

CARCANET PRESS LTD
Alliance House, 30 Cross Street
Manchester M2 7AQ
www.carcanet.co.uk

A CIP catalogue record for this book is available from
the British Library, ISBN 9781784102807

The publisher acknowledges financial assistance
from Arts Council England.

Contents

III

IV

Translations from Seán Ó Ríordáin

Translations from Lorca

I

'Long is the way and hard, that out of Hell leads up to light.'

John Milton, *Paradise Lost*

The Angel of Camden Street

After the funeral I found him in Camden Street
I knew him by the wings, the missing teeth.

He stood three feet high with a mad grin
Sweeney, if he'd been Indonesian.

I paid him off and carted him back to the flat
On the last instalment, hid him in the car boot

Until we got home. He found his plinth
On a high stool in a corner. Half nymph

Half hermaphrodite. Dinner guests pointed out
He had female parts and looked crazed.

I hadn't noticed these angelic aspects,
Neither the stylized hair nor flat painted breasts.

As for the red lips, a few anatomical oddities –
Heavenly bodies come in all shapes and sizes.

O half-angel, half-bowsprit, you're all I've got to send out
To guard Dermot in his trawler, caught in a force eight

Night flying over Sligo, or ashore, Lear on the rocks
Scourge of angle-grinding tourists. You can come back

When he tumbles late into heaven at the feet
Of some martyr saying, 'I thought there'd be a serpent'

And the Blessed Virgin looks up and asks,
'Now who in the Lord is that?'

Elpenor

Sing how the woman held out a glass
Brimming with light. How the prisoner drank it.
How it tasted angelic and black. That he got drunk
And fell off the roof – yes Elpenor destroyed
But it could have been otherwise.
What if Odysseus – always easily delayed –
Had turned back when he missed his friend
And buried him with his armour where he fell.
Would we know his name without his year in hell?

January Aubade

FOR OISIN

Hold out for the morning poem,
A raw daub of light in the east, the moon
Still fading through rain that has not stopped

For months, the mad-making wind
And the sky close as a torturer's hood, tight
As a vice. Hold out for the flake of white.

Keep driving into it until black rain yields
To the pale shimmer, the mind's shield.
This is your birthright, lustre

A scapular to face down midwinter.
Fields will be sketched in, and people.
Colour will seep back into the world.

Keep driving until a door opens
And open it will – like when a theorem
Slides into place, or the subjunctive, a click

Of gears shifting up in the flick
Of a cat's tail – and light pulses
A small galaxy through the glass

That releases slowly the mind hurt
From its ceaseless interrogation
In the unfriendly dark and opens it.

Breaking into Silence

There are daily offices,
The feel of timber
On the soles of the feet
Stepping downstairs

Water gushing cold
Into the plastic kettle.
The first cup ritual
As communion, sipped.

Rehearsals do not work.
Words become audience.
They make too much noise
Or sulk or don't turn up.

They are in those ways odd
Yoking us to habit
To monkish obedience.
They tolerate no other Gods.

They give no 'A's for effort.
When we deviate the roses sicken.
The heart has to be in on it
Sniffing the air, red-pelted.

The self idling, parked.
Acids and the dyes we live by
Corrode or stain our hands.
They hurt us, but not into poetry.

The Walk

The heavy clouds barrack me into a square,
Harvest is a sentence in chequered solitaire.

We walk Knockranny Hill and it's lights-up
On the iceberg. Haws, mountain ash, rose hip.

The late scabious is mauve-eyed to match
Those little lines and circles on the fuselage

And wings of painted butterflies that perch
Tilted with hatpins on their slim necks.

We are a year married and a sudden look
Reminds me why, even though you woke me up

Singing hymns about pilgrims and goblins
Yesterday, saying *don't you know Bunyan*

When I complained, even though you retrieve
Bank statements from the bin and make me read them.

I am afraid of autumn. You like it.
Season of mellow fruitfulness and all that.

In Connemara? Stone roses. The days are dished out.
Thin slices lie half eaten on my plate.

You say 'Let's look at flights.' We walk
To where the sea shines. It cures and mocks.

Flight tracks criss-cross to New York and Spain.
The sky is twenty fathoms high. It's wild goose time.

Harvest

In this light it's all tin retábulos,
A pewter vase out of *Still Life with Pigeons*
Dead-feathered as an old pan
My morning rages for the sun.

A trout backsliding under the bridge
Swallows light through his skin.
Grey shears off the river, a ridge
Of scales, the bladed wind scraping them.

It is all reverse increments,
Days taken in like a consumptive's skirts.
I'm all for letting out, March
The gear shift of the vernal equinox.

Which is lighter, a ton of feathers
Or a ton of lead? Lead, of course
What's a ton of feathers but a Universe
Of dark stuff squeezed between your fingers.

When the rivers rush forward again
A tortured salmon springs, jackknives
The waterfall, fins whirring. The moon
Fish-eyed, hatches small grey pearls.

He is making for a country not his.
It has always owned him. There, autumn is brief.
Sunlight cascades out of a hard sky, not this
Spent light, leaden, flat as a fishknife.

I'd rather be at the fish-houses,
The cold already burning, a raw bar
Matching the machines' clatter
'Go down ye blood red roses'.

The de Burgo Chalice

This was the marriage of a foreign man
To a native woman, to weld two clans.

There was precedence. Since Strongbow
There were wives that kept their own names.

Religion helped. Did she, the first Gráinne,
Believe any of it, God or the fairy?

He taught her hawking and pleasure,
Endowed an Abbey, coped with her temper.

She swam for him. They were rich,
Young, married. Grace and Thomas.

Overhead history gathered.
Underfoot, the ground shifted.

Latin came in with the Roman church
Hiberniores Hibernis ipsis

Men at their conquests
But was it love, even so?

At evening lapwings and curlews
Called, sweet even in the servants' hovels

With their squalor, their indentured lives
Brutal and short. Whimbrels

Echoed in the silver cup, plain
As the blue harebell, printed with their names.

The Chalice II

They lived and died, Gráinne and Thomas
Married. Around them, the numerous unwritten

Were walked on, used, occasionally admired
Fine as the honey-smelling machair.

The higher-ups arranged things,
Suited action to purpose, love sometimes.

The old way, sacrifice in a chalice
And *Hiberniores, Hibernii ipsis*.

Show Day

There are bright stars, the odd comet; night aeroplanes
Criss-cross this vast parish. They tell the time.
A blue shark breaks the sky over the lake. It rains.

Below the gable, white horses fan out. They are at home
Ploughing under the moon. Each knows
His own name and speaks it in a language half mine.

Last night they broke cover or I surprised them – horses
After all sense danger. Waking from a dream
I went to the window. They were standing close

To the house, all facing South. They stared, then ran
Without a sound, manes streaming to race or catch
The tide. Those things are not unheard of here where even

The horses emigrate. At such junctures worlds ratchet,
Directions change. Traffic streams through space.
People come back for a look, bothered by what they left

Which is dearer to them than a bushel of science
And all the Wild West spindrift on TV. They miss their votes,
The smell off rotting seaweed, the sight of horses.

The horses are spreading in drifts. They grow freely
As if the rock spawned them, the last locals
Unendangered, idled, wedded to the sea.

Weather

The house sits on the hill
Washing its face in the sun
Humping its back against rain.
It stays where it is, reliable
And has never yet fallen down
In spite of provocation.

When I walked the rooms at night
In the blue dressing gown
Old silk from Camden town
It held me. When I went away
I moved through those rooms
Touching things, making sure.

Back again, gales blow for three days.
I watch them move in.

Dominion

To keep their trammelled wilderness
They are re-wilding the parks
With deer and predators.

Such pain as we punish the animals
With our notions. Some fools
Are starting it all again like gods

Then green herbs for meat
Man *in his image*, dominion granted
As the snake slips through the grass

Ignorant of the first separation
Of light from dark, air from water
The comet from the eye of the tiger.

Scarce

The future is water – plastic
Famine drums, a dented kettle,
A brushed-steel tap
Set in tombstone marble
In a slim kitchen.
Water, cleaned, dirty, chlorinated,
A dry river. Heat waves at the Arctic.
Cut off means war.
It is oil, it is diamonds.
The poem and the soil demand it.

Uilleann

FOR BRIAN BOURKE

People sometimes get drunk on the music.
One early morning after the night
Before not having finished, the story
Goes that when a baby started crying
His father picked him up, tucked his bellows
Under his elbow and started playing him
Along with two fiddles, a tin whistle
And the piper who tuned in to the baby's cries
For the 'Walls of Limerick'.

When the baby, sick of the noise, stopped
They were half way through 'Shoe the Donkey'
And seeing that it did no harm swung
Into a storm of jigs, the baby squawking
'Saddle the Pony'.
That boy is a slave now to fiddle,
Harp, melodeon. Somehow in all those tunes
He learned to listen for his own note.
He lives on inland water where sound
Whether the listener hears or not
Is magnified and separate and moves
Over the air like a sky goat's bleat.

He avoids the pipes. He has his reasons.
He has heard the story
Of the octopus who was locked into a room
For a week to practise.
When they let him out the pipes had learned
To play the octopus.
The thing about musicians is
They respond to glory.

What Ireland needs

Is not more moneymen or oil companies
She does not need more laboratories
Administrators, or doctors.

She does not need more lawyers
Or offices or post office boxes
Or chairs of Funny Business in Universities.
She does not need more inspectors
Of prisons, septic tanks, drains
Nor more giant windmills to subdue Connaught
And annexe Spain.

What Ireland needs
In every government department
Is an incredible dancing man
To play the bones for civil servants
Secretaries, nurses, number crunchers
On his thighs, his wrists, his jiggling hips
On their clavicles and elbows
All along the old trapezium
Down across their rude computers
Up their mandibles and sternum
With a flourish of the skeletons.

A wild whirly man to put pep in their step
And teach them what's what
And in homage to Yeats and Aristotle
Beat the taws upon their bottoms.

Tory

FOR LILLIS Ó LAOGHAIRE

We'll take off for Tory
In the ship of fools
With a mast half cut, spools
Of carnival bulbs, lit. Roary
Rory at the helm,
Your only man in a storm.

Tory has the mandate of song.
On a rock in the middle of the ocean
We'll mock dead autumn
And sing through the worst
Winter can throw at us.
Put a sock in the laments.

Báidín Fheidhlimidh
Will take us to Tory. We'll be sure
Of a welcome if we keep in tune.
There's a king and a lifeboat.
There's a dog that swims with a dolphin
The Republic of Tory is what's left.

Fame

Pythagoras worked out his theorem
From a tune. The symmetry hit him at a session
Afterhours and 'Have ye no homes to go to'
Down among the woods of Babylonio.

He called the tune on the old triangles
For a few thousand years
And worked out how to vex schoolchildren
With 'a's and 'b's squared, cooked and eaten.

If not Pythagoras some musical Babylonian
History has ignored or forgotten,
Someone whose thunder he took by stealth
As Dylan borrowed from Woody's wealth.

Lyre strings measuring the vibrations
Pythagoras mastered the variations
Leaving hordes of schoolgirls giddy as kite tails
Hanging, goldfingered and smitten.

Posy

Those gentians I promised not to –
I hid three between the leaves
And yesterday on my knees
I came across them in the rubbish
Where so much starts. They washed
The house in quantum blue.

II

'What are the roots that clutch, what branches grow
Out of this stony rubbish?'

T. S. Eliot, *The Wasteland*

Beeches

So this is what the brouhaha, the fuss,
Autumn leaves turning, green shoots,
Birds, all the slightly creepy
Metaphors for girls is all about.

Even their winter shape
Is out of sync. Too big, too thick-boned
Like the giants they are. Too tall, too old
For this thin soil. They hulk.

They lock light out. They sulk
Even in summer. No sun gets past.
I have made an uneasy truce
With their gloom but it sucks me in.

Time trudges through them, school clocks
Running slow. They have no voice
Only that spring Elizabethan show
Intrinsically decent, out of place.

The Tree

FOR MARINA CARR

'Have you no pity then?
Once we were men
Now we are stumps of wood'

Dante, translated by Robert Pinsky

Last year a tree punched five holes
In the roof, smashed through
Windows, a glasshouse, the porch.

Its twin at the gate stood too long
Old and sickening, half alien
Half thundercloud. Now it is down.

A chainsaw-juggling acrobat
Swung up through the branches
And cut it to a gibbet

That he felled with the precision
Of a rocket launch. The floor
Shook. That night stars sprang

Like daisies where the great beech
Had been. The world was all dazzle
And my breath, held for too long

Flowed again. A sharp grief
Surprised me next morning
To see life ended with the limbs hacked off.

Its time was over. There will be
Other trees, slim and limber, birch
Silver and light-friendly.

A tree fallen is not the same
As a tree felled. What am I to make of it
With its imperial scansion?

Who knows what the tree wants – a happy death?
The Welsh say the first tablets were timber
The woods' hierarchy etched on beech.

I tell myself it had no purchase here
In the thin soil, blasted by gales
Roots loosed and rotted, a nightmare

Where harpies nested and snapped twigs bled.
Now it is timber, rhymed, end-stopped,
Ready to be transformed

Into something simple, a desk or breakfast bar.
A bad dream dragged into daylight
And hewn into a table and chairs.

Tree II

Not long after you were planted
My train broke down in another language.

Its syntax knotted like blackthorn
Yielded bright poems on a black bough.

What am I bar fear and admiration
To make of you? I take no joy

In your downfall but look at how
The tree-shaped brightness dances.

Tree III

When I was small trees grew wild
In saltwater. They came in on the tide
For roof beams, a chair for a child.

I had a fiddle carved from windfall.
When the bow scraped out a few tunes
A sweeter note echoed under the keel.

Woodland

Victorian. Sycamore. 'Very pretty.'
I expect Virginia's demon underthings
To half emerge – 'Ghastly' –
Below the rational trees.
This is how the trained mind plants.

The tales that briars breed
Are not obedient. The dwarf swapped
When a stray hand reached
For the child, the red apple, poisoned.
Fairies and dragonflies stay away
Pinned in their blue hazed fancy.

November

The skeletal arms of a tree
What do I see? Eyes open
A low hill capped in rain
A woodcut of purgatory.
With my eyes closed, the sea.

Chess

A tree. The rising sea gaining on
The last oak plantation.

After each storm, a bright quilt
Thrown over the traffic grid-locked

Over burger wrappings, needles, boys.
A shroud for the bodies in doorways.

But it's only rain, a slick that reflects
Glitter from a weak sun, fun's wreckage.

The sea holds back for another season
Her long dance with the moon.

The Hare

I'm back with my long ears
And leverets. In spring
I box for a sweetheart
Box with my sweetheart
And dance like Nijinsky
Otherwise I'm shy.

Old rites. Old as my strong back legs
Leftover legs with a spring in them
And my long ears for beauty.
Strange, some think, prehistoric
But once I heard it said
I have the shape of a hermit's poem.

The Raven

Blue-black on your catwalk.
Augur and peck. There is a conspiracy
Of you over my head in your black
Priests' dresses. Go back
To whoever sent you from the cave
Near the volcano. I do not want
Your warning or your news
Or the hard husks of your calls.

The Rat

I am hunted, hated, feared.
They revile my children
Set cats and small dogs
To torture me. I too am born.
I too live and do little harm.
I only eat what is left.
They hate me because
I am the late-night traffic
In their sleeping heads.

I am a child of the river
And lake. Not even the monk
Gave me one good deed.
He let the otter rescue
The holy psalter for Ronan.
I could have done that.

They sent me out among the junkies
And rubbish sacks, into the gaol cells.
I will be here when the seas rise
And cover their carcasses.
There will be ravens feasting
On the next hill. Hating. Still hating.

I wanted none of it, their curses
Or their rows, or their bloody gods.

Wolf

Meanwhile the wolf guards
What is left to him, the last cry
Elusive as an echo. The gods

Are leaving, or have left and this
Is Echo, waiting for him to speak
First so that she can show herself.

He sticks his snout in the water. Ice
Darts in his eyes like a fish.
Swift like the river he circles

And closes on nothing. He howls
The great open vowel of his need
And hears her answering call.

Fox

On the bridge
Over the waterfall
A she-fox pauses.
A salmon springs,
Falls back, spent
As a two-bob bit.

Hah! The vixen barks
Once in the moonlight
And passes. None of it
Matters to her.
The river's roar
The fish beating

Upriver, driven
By the old compulsion,
The woman savaged
By her pack of dreams.
She is the moon's red beauty
Freed from pity.

Bird Anonymous

The bird was grey as an overgrown dove
And took off out of the river.
Note that it wasn't floating but stood
On a submerged rock. From above

It was a cloak opening, a landlocked skate
Feathered, unzipping the cold day
Making its escape unclassified.
Unnamed bird, the one that got away.

Firs

'The name you call us is not our name'
Michael Hartnett

Firs sang for Sibelius, formal iced
Wearing the green sap of Finland.

Here they are mute, except to creak
In the wind like a lost corncrake.

Dark wardens, their green uniform
Blues like sloes. Touch and the skin

Prickles and hardens. Telegraph-pole-thin
Evergreen, they offer nothing.

Spiders thrive among the fretted spears
Birds claim reluctant shelter.

From Michael's book the green gold came:
The name I call them is not their name.

The black swans have had their silence
And peck out old names among the cones

A last symphony for dead myths
Before new blood waters the ashes.

Time out of Mind

The eyes see. The mind interprets. What feels?
The soul? Soul is good enough. It has lasted,
Stood the test of many translations, slippery as an eel.
It is five to seven. There are three of us in the big pool.
Waiting for the clock. It is as calm as sunrise.
The surface is unbroken. The minute tiles
Are blue, a sky with patterns of thick T-bars
Laid regularly in black
A man tests the water with a small kick.

The T-bar in his lane ripples and bulges,
Then writhes, an apothecary snake.
The water stills and it becomes singular again,
Itself. Or is it? So much for observation.
One small kick and a line becomes a sugar stick.
This has implications. Take it too far
And the mind dissolves. The T-bar doesn't.
Even a physicist needs certainties:
'Philosophy is dead.' 'There is no God.'

After all, there must be frontiers,
Territories to be explored, minerals exploited.
Who but painters and the mad
Can live with all the possibilities
Whirling like galaxies. Not even God
Who separated dark from light,
Land from water. Cadmus from Harmony
By marriage, granted.
Someone invented M-theory. Holy, holy, holy.

A fairytale particle to tie it all together
The suffering, the marvels and the glory
Of the first clean dive, the vee of joined fingers
Cleaving the surface, then turbulence. Captive
The mind rides the whirligig as best it can
Or is unseated and pitched down among the harpies
Scourged. The road up is hard and long. This
Is when the trout appears with your gold ring
In his mouth. O! A shining vocative.

Dreampoems

i

The dream again – that real place
The paint flaking on the walls
Old walls that had seen Mallarmé
Walk by with Rimbaud and Verlaine
And knew enough of death
And dreams, their disturbed vision
Still insisting on arranging the blue
Scarf of evening just so – that man's face
In a mirror half askew by the doorway
Here in this place is an invasion.

It may be his death
Showing his freshest side.
It may be nothing.

ii

No one will know who I am
From what I have written.
There was an obstacle.

I was not free to tell the stories
With an end, beginning, middle
And to tell the truth, these
Didn't interest me. Between
One thing and another, truth
Glints in the rock pools.
It darts and burrows in the sand
With its long claws.

I have netted a few beauties
Some crayfish, a lobster.
I have learned to handle
Those creatures with caution
With my rough asbestos gloves.

Sometimes I am lucky
A child is born
And the truth is good to touch
Fresh as a June mushroom

iii

Look, he said, dreams are dreams
They are not real. A chair, a table
A room – those are solid.
She thinks that rooms mutate
And get smaller as we grow
Bigger and if this goes too far
Things go into reverse
And what cannot be contained shrinks.

So a boy, fully grown, is now the size
Of a thumb. They know he has shrunk.
They wait for him at the station.
Where his father
With great fuss and complication
Is to pick them all up. He is not there.
She searches along the wainscoting
And cannot find him

This boy who is imprinted in her blood
Lives inside her head and somewhere
Deliberately or not, is now invisible,
Lost, unavailable and she fumbles
With some text or connection
To tell his father he is not here yet
Because he has shrunk and this is not
His fault or hers and not deliberate

To please wait but the keys will not connect.
Dreams are nightmares, real or not.

Sweeney

i

It comes on him and ebbs
As the power of the goddess
Rose and fell in Achilles
On waves of madness.

The severing of mind and magic
When power shifts
Exacts new tributes. He thinks
The new regime spreads panic.

When the curse worked in him
And pin-feathered his skin
He did not in his agony
Put to sea where he is easy

Or when he dived into the salt
The blue glass green glass
Clear eyed wash of it, he didn't stay –
He still craves human company.

ii

He's back again, perching thin-shanked
In the trees, roosting out on the islands
In full flight like a cock pheasant
Ragged from battle, a splendid eejit.

His feathers are grey, dragging and tarry
From the rubbish tips, the madness
In full black fire burning up his nights
The whirligig sky mocking and starry

Watching him, eyes red from pain
And the pitiful bare shanks
I know torment. This is tattered man.
I know he is afraid of the dank lake

He will fly to in the spring
Cycling the air wildly to get ahead
Of what preys on him and crying
Hoarse prayers into the void.

And somehow he has not ended it
Sweeney Agonistes, the Beautiful.
Sweeney Redivivus, the Magnificent
Old pagan, waiting for a miracle.

iii

Now his tribe are scattered everywhere
Destroyed with needles
The not-good-enough boys
And girls dancing across the weir

Walking by any deep fast water
That will drown the voices
So they can sleep to the soothing clatter
Of blue willow teacups and dishes.

In the City

Nothing menaces my sleep here.
I am not startled awake when a screech
Of cats threatens to enter my door.

There are footsteps on the stairs
A fumbled creak down the corridor
Lovers arriving singly or in pairs.

When night and day separate
Like a peach around six
I am sleeping beyond harm's reach.

Night in the city teems with Rimbaud's own.
Fingers slip quietly into pockets
Of youths X-ray-pale under the neon.

Knives flash like eels in alleyways.
High up a silent jet slices the moon
Looking in windows, guarding our dreams.

III

'Lights all askew in the Heavens
Stars not where they seemed
Or were calculated to be
But nobody need worry.'

Cable to the *New York Times* announcing
Einstein's theory of relativity

First Visit to Penn's Landing

There's been no sea for months so the river,
A slow tide of gunmetal, provides a link
To two hundred miles away and the Maine Coast
With its rock pools and a mermaid
Gathering barnacles and Cal on his legacy:
'I want them to say I was a heartbreaker.'
A mermaid with hands torn from the rough shells.
Trouble from allergies is *de rigueur* here
And it could be that the silver in her ring
With its single black stone is laced with zinc.

The water is icy, too cold, and it stings
But its sting is glorious and it strikes me
As a kind of explanation for the America
That is protestant and white or the start
Of one. A training ship *The Gazela*
Fished for cod in Newfoundland
And the cold shores of Greenland
And in the heat of New Orleans she starred
In a movie with vampires on board.

The river is flat, wide, undammed and why
It should warm me with this small truth
In winter, with the taste of hard-won *bacahlau*
And the drink still standing in a bar in New Orleans
Unclaimed as the future, is how life's promises
Reward us for keeping faith
With all the atoms whirling in a word, with the lights
In spinning tops. It's why we keep going to the circus
With our high-wire acts, this chance meeting
With the elements of our own make-up floating free.

Natives

English is making strange again
Contrary as a two-year-old silence
Irish sticks its tongue out, in
Hard necessary syllables that spit and hiss
And consonants like shards of gneiss.
English is not the tool for this
But English is what I have.

This is no way to map this frozen place
The sharp light, cars like barges, the flat
Lean grant of William Penn's tamed share
Rearing suddenly up a hundred floors
Vertical but mapping is not what I am at.
Not sap, sap, sapping but naming.
Where is the voice of the Indian?

I hear it in the wind, feel it flense
The skin, strip the wires, buckle
The ground under the asphalt. The howl
Of America grown distant, the tense
Ghosts in street-corner faces. A fox
Cried last night outside our window
For a mate   for food   the native for no.

The Ghost Chant

What is it to be a people
That lived so lightly on the land
Their own families named
Each of them for the simple traits
They carried or would inherit
As gifts upon becoming grown,
To grow up young.

What it must be to lose
An entire continent to men
Who traded in baubles and lies
Who flourished under false names
And then to see your trails
Cobwebbed in the moonlight, pale
Crossed by ghost caravans.

They were stitched between mountains
Across the river we call Delaware
Night raiders, ghost encampments.
What I am hunting is the syllables
Of old names. I hear their echoes
In the chant, electrifying the body
Drumming, singing the wolf's story.

On Showing *The Dead* at Villanova

It seems now I will always recall their faces
And remember each name: Elizabeth, Julia, Devon,
Oliver, with his chalk and cheese grandfathers,
Names slightly formal, like the film.

The young women despised Gabriel at first.
He was, said one, self-centred and worse
Lacking in emotional intelligence.
Mr Brown was creepy, the aunts feisty and frail.

A high-end dinner party, they said. I stopped
The action half-way and asked them to guess
The second half. All things possible, all different.
Next class, they were, they said, surprised.

Of the film, their reviews were mixed.
The boy concentrated on technical terms
The girls on Gretta, thrown on the bed.
They liked Gabriel more now, her less.

I told them Huston was on oxygen.
When it came to the snow, the formal journey
Across the central plain
Their faces had the look of Gretta on the stairs.

They were more impressed with Joyce's story,
The sharp twist of the boy's death, than the movie.
I wanted to say 'Don't look back.
Stay here, where West means hope, not death.'

A Singing Supper

FOR PAUL MULDOON

Bagpipe music there was none
At the White Dog Cafe though a baby
Gave a fair imitation briefly.
Someone said get a gun. It stopped. O Mercy.

Poetry dipped in and out
Among the charcuterie and Madame Blavatsky
Somewhat like Marianne Moore
In the picture on the menu
Like a bat out of hell herself.
Off with her leg the surgeons said
Which is what surgeons do
And what can you expect
But the lady, not for turning
Said off with you, my leg
Will not go to the spirit world
Before me, are you mad
And lay a white dog across it
And was cured.

Hogwash maybe but this hog
Was clean and raised green
And ended as excellent pork terrine.
I'd swear it said 'Eat me'. O Alice.

We named the dead first, then the living
Enquired after trawlers and family and tennis
Checked in on Moycullen and the Moy
And who had a book out every ten minutes
And who a film, admiringly.

Later I thought about Ireland
How we're better away
Than going back, mostly
But through the evening what I wanted to say
And didn't, between the word *kind*
And the word *lightly*
Was about the French translator who
Unable to imagine anyone
Going to sightsee a roundabout
Came out with
The Ballygawley Carousel
(I wanted someone to sing it)
And how a few always attract
The whirligig roustabout music
To their poems like Rimbaud
And others don't
Or kill it.

Sentence

Something about America
Is good for us
Frank O'Hara's lunchtimes
The public road, skies
High as kites.

Send your poets out
Early and often in chain gangs
To listen to the jazz chants
The beat, the out of the head
Into the feet blues, the trail of tears
Outer space size of what can be said
Where envelopes are pushed and lines
Stretch open to negotiation, long and generous.

Franglais

They gave us chic and soigné and farouche
You gave them weekend, posh and chips.
They gave us louche.

Gotham Dusk Poem

The first thing you notice is the crocodile.
Her skin is wrinkled and green but that is not
Unusual here. She wears a diamond bracelet
And there's something wonky about her walk.
Six-inch heels do that, especially if you're past
Eighty. She doesn't care. She's shopping for shades
The old-fashioned diamond-studded pointy ones
Are in again after forty years and she liked them then.

Batman strides towards us. People take no notice.
This is his town. He hasn't aged but maybe
He's had work done and the crocodile is Lois Lane.
He's on the phone, arguing. 'Jesus, Tommy, hang on...'
Who argues with Batman? And Tommy? Who knew?

Further on a poor man is putting all the rubbish
Into his shopping trolley. He is dressed in character.
As we pass he puts his arm around the bin afraid
Someone will steal it from him. His face
Has the sly look of a beaten child, or Estragon
Struggling against his terrible silence
But he's no actor. He has no hat, no comic turn.

It's getting dark and the lights come up. Look up,
Up, up! There's a car on top of the Chrysler, silver-tipped.
Down here, a yellow dog is lying in a window
Reading a book, an old paperback
Under a standard lamp with a faded shade,
Not drawing attention to itself. Down here
In Zen City where the ordinary people live.

Fairytale, New York

There is a second skin, another life
She is riffling through garments on a rail
Hangers clacking like train tracks
On her face the absorption women reserve

For important rituals, birthing a child,
Make-up, shopping. She is looking for a myth
To wear. It must be simple, well made
And fit as well as the old one, which

She has outgrown and never chose.
Somehow she picked it up, as she passed
In a hurry and never really knew whose
Hand-me-down it was or that it wouldn't last.

She has just stepped out of it, in another place.
She looked at those rails several times before
And went back to a new version of the old dress,
A fake tiara and a cat thrown over the shoulder

For opera occasions. You're Antigone
Or you're Electra, said Mother Sugar. In physics
All the possibilities are true, said Feynman.
She passes over the red silk, the white homespun

For a scaled pelt in rust and silver
Something to match the river's
Steel sheen in the city when she roams
At night, unafraid, anonymous.

Occupation

We are the stutterers.
The speech of liars pours out
While we mumble and fill in.
We give the wrong information
Or none at all because
The questions make no sense.
In the language of the surveyors
We are dumb. Our tongues
Blunt like knives in drawers
Too long unused. They are fluent
And make the rules but we only need
To win once, like freedom fighters
With a song that blows the house down
Or up, if that is your tune.

My Boss Vasques

Each of us has a boss
Vanity, Fame, Fear
Of Madness. Some people
Work for Failure
All their lives.

I prefer the tangible
So I work for Vasques
At the Arts Council
Designing surveys
Shaped like Greek vases.

Arrival. Possession. A City.

The station. A man with a briefcase at night,
Aged thirty-two, hungry as a wolf. Streets polished
With rain. A woman steps off a waterbus.
His tourist guide, nutria coated, a goddess.
Ariadne evades him. She goes home
To her husband, leaving him alone.
Joseph Brodsky in Venice on the pull. Outsmarted.
It is windy and the air stinks of seaweed.

That, you might think, was the end of romance
But for seventeen years between heart attacks
He comes back to a city he can never possess
because to him the smell of frozen seaweed
Was happiness, a deep cloud of loosed
Molecules into which he stepped
And met himself. The rest, perfume, lace,
Her new marriage in the Mid-West – mere surface.

Literary Life

The savagery of poets lodges
Not in the heart or the soul
But in the gizzard, in what's left
Of the soft liver, under the nails.

Marianne Moore didn't like Sylvia
But adored Ted. The spinster
With her witch feathers, her witch hat
Her Morrigan heart.

She gave him the prize
But returned Sylvia's offerings,
Her blue veined poems, saying *'They seem
Valuable copies.*

I will not engross them.' The spur
Worked its way deep under Ted's skin
Until it lodged safely in the spleen for years
And came out glistening with gall.

Star

She is resentful and forbidden as a French nun.
Her landlocked face looks West and South.
Inland the lakes shiver and spring shut like traps.
Unless she snaps her painted fingers
Got up to the nines in Parthian red
It will all will flash past, into the ice-blue world
Of beautiful solutions, into the brilliance
Of space and antimatter or it could be that she dies
Young and in her dancing shoes. Berenice.

If not, what of late middle age's unsolved
Equations, her deepening knowledge
Of planetary silence and the cold sea of antiparticles.
Who wants her now in her nuclear pelt
Or vows reversed, stuck in some golf club in Spain
With a new husband down to his last ten
Housing estates, a husband she might one day knife
And streaming past her crackling hairbrush, life.

Heroine

Albertine again. And look, he said,
Who would have thought
When she saw the signs of the disease
She was carrying in herself
She'd commit the great sacrifice
And withdraw from the world
A hermit, wasting away alone –
Albertine, who loved to party.
He shook his head in admiration –
His lover with her freight of sickness
Doing him proud
Leaving the city without force.
Imagine, he said, her bravery. Such class.

Ballyconneely

They are not big-feeling people
They did not go after prizes
Or boast, except for the woman
In the next village, known as the Queen.
When strangers mentioned Hy Brasil
They let on not to know its name

But spoke only of an island
That sank and appeared, sank
Again every seven years
Or so they were told, they said
To be polite and not disappoint.

Among themselves they said
'Did you ever hear tell of Atlantis?'
One said seafóid but agreed
There might be something in it,
One said odd there was no sign
Of ghosts after television.

It was all a cod put out by priests
And druids to keep us down.
What they told to strangers
Were not lies, just a simple version
To excite them and keep them happy.

Thus was rhyming Herodotus known
As the Father of History
And at the same time the Father of Lies
When he only heard
What he wanted to hear
Which became static when he wrote it down.

Peace Walk

In Israel in the town of X a man walks
Each morning to the end of his street
Where the desert begins. It is how he wakes
Standing just before sunrise, the air cold and sweet.

He does this to feel the dark and gather his calm
For the talk he must have with his neighbour
A retired colonel who sees the next holocaust slam
In from every direction, and for the day's labour.

He also walks after sunset and stops outside
To listen to a nocturne played well by a young girl.
He mentions that instead of peace and the old man's pride
Softens him – his daughter's daughter, so musical.

Reading this, the good habit of taking peace
Where we find it, knowing it will be scorched by noon
And holding it inside our dark cistern
Makes more sense than roadmaps. Walk on, Amos Oz.

Echoes

FOR STEVE

If as Verlaine believed a woman's feet send
Echoes through the heads of unhappy men
In buttoned up tiny ankle boots
Or on the same ankles a pair of rough sabots

I wonder at the oiled grooves a man's mind
Travels on, how the cogs once set in motion find
The path of least resistance leads to echoes
Of women they have loved down to their toes.

I see yours, the way you wear the heel down
More on the right than left, the outside lean
The slight crease a grain above the toes.
For a tall man you are not hard on shoes.

Bellini's Pietà

For this mother it is a short flight
Between the adoration of the child
And Good Friday, all Saturday night
And not a wound in the house washed.

She is the woman we used to mock
For sitting at the foot of the cross
And him for getting himself killed
To fulfil a book – all madness

Because the son thought he was God.
We knew nothing. She tended
The body, numbered hair, limbs.
Hands strengthened by work

Hold her dead son up.
We had our saving jab of ignorance but
She knew the joy he brought
Was mortgaged from the start.

Changeling

No there were no fairies.
There were riders on grey horses
Stealing the living child
Swapping him with their own.

There were no princes, no heroes.
No old woman spat
On the baby's head for luck
But a thrush sang at midnight.

There was dead moon, a zinc night
There was a howl in her throat
A mother cursed
The day she was born.

There was a black horse
A man dismounted
A red grin – she went with him
For excitement.

When the house broke open
All shell and skin
Like a duck's egg, she roared in pain
Like a man in warp spasm

But she made no sound.
Her mind closed into a fist.
There, blasted on the ground
Her dolls, the bed and all the rest.

The Bad Mother

If you keep up the story of the good mother
Someone is soon going to dream a bad mother
Then they are going to punish their nightmares,
Lock them outside the fortress, refuse to answer
The bell, the door.

She is changed in fairytales to the father's wife. No stain
Attaches to the real mother, safely dead.
What of the bad mother with her sheaf of sins
Mortal as poems, crying, crying, calling her daughters
Turned to stone.

She wants God to take some blame, to tell her
Freud didn't know everything, he was a snake-oil man.
She wants what we all want, to be shriven
If there's no priest in the confessional box,
Then television.

Forgotten

So this is how it feels to be God's mother – adored.
The devil had a mother too and she raised him well
Was, as they say, good enough. Went to trouble.
No mother is ever good enough until she's dead.

What could you do? He was an angel
Until the teenage years – rough companions
He ran wild. Those boys were demons
Running across the midnight hill.

She gets the praise, the adoration. Her dead son
Broken in her arms. No one remembers
The bad thief's mother. Gestas – full of anger.
If I'd claimed him they'd have cut me down.

It's not that simple. He was kind and had grey eyes.
Something got into him – drink, politics. Damn the breath
That killed him. He was my son to the last. Visions?
I hated his death. I will not agree with his death.

IV

Translations from Seán Ó Ríordáin

THIS LANGUAGE HALF WITH ME

Who tied this knot between us
Half tame, half owned tongue?
There's a want in every line
Unless you make me your own.

There's another one beside you
And she's asking me home.
I'm caught between the two of you
And it's tearing me apart.

Unless I keep you with me
Stroking your fur
I'll be robbed of your sanctuary
And you'll lose me forever.

A half heart does no one any good.
I'll just have to give in to you
Though you're playing hard to get
My tuning-fork language, half understood.

AFTER SENDING HIM TO THE DOGHOUSE

Don't be at me like this, dog,
be glad I drove you from this life,
you were my noblest welcoming friend,
though it was me that had to end your days.

You're on your own now, hound
if you're still a dog and not a shade,
surrounded by enemies without mercy
as you wait for the death wound.

Your big dog heart was always loyal,
nothing in it but love
but the ones you loved betrayed you
faraor géar, and you an old stray.

You had the ways of a house dog
With the deference of the stray.
Now all that's left of your bounding love
Is here in my sore heart tonight.

THE GIANTS

Like thunderbolts, the pain descending,
Waves of it.
I can hack this. This is nothing
I tell myself.

Morning will bring ease
But the sun has risen
And the pain – Jesus, I'm broken
Every cell stitched to the cross.

The pains are plural and arguing.
I am their subject now.
I contain every verb and noun
In their lexicon

They chew my flesh and suck
The sap from my veins.
I am their well-mannered host,
Humble and meek.

They have won the day.
I lost.
The enemy is in the house. Patience
and I'll wait my chance.

No. This pain is tearing me apart.
As I surrender
I let out a wild scream
And my soul rises in wonder

I scream against God.
Do your worst, Christ,
Let loose every pain in the armoury.
I'm finished.

Like rain, solace descending
And strength.
I make out two giants side by side
The scream, and God.

CLAUSTROPHOBIA

Beside my glass of red wine
is a candle, and panic.
The image of Our Lord stares
powerless as a plaster saint.
What's left of the night
floods the yard.
Night rules outside the window.
If the candle quenches
in spite of me
the shadows will jump
into my lungs.
My mind will sink
terror will choke me
and make of me the night.
I will become the living dark.
    But let the candle last
    this one night
    I will become the republic of light
    until day takes over.

Translations from Lorca

THE GYPSY NUN

Silence of myrtle and lime
Mallow between the slim grasses.
The nun is embroidering wallflowers
On a straw-coloured altarcloth.
A prism of seven coloured birds
Are flying through the grey candelabra.
In the distance the church growls
Like a bear on its back.
How well she sews. With such grace!
She'd like to embroider
The tea-coloured cloth
With the flowers of her fancy.
Such a sunflower that would be!
And a spangled magnolia with ribbons
Such saffron and moons scattered on the altarcloth.
Five citrons are ripening
In a kitchen nearby
And five fuchsias
Cut in Almería.

Two horsemen gallop
Through the nun's vision.
A late breeze stirs her shirt.
She looks up at the clouds and hills
In the frozen distance
Her heart breaks
Her sugar-and-verbena heart.
She sees the high plain
With its twenty suns.
In her vision

Rivers flow uphill.
Still she goes on with her flowers
While bars of light play chess
In the breeze
On the high lattice window.

SONG OF THE BLACKS IN CUBA

At the rising of the moon I'm off
To Santiago de Cuba.
In a coach of blackwater
I'm off to Santiago
Where the palm trees will be singing
As they swing above the rooftops
I'm going to Santiago.
When the palm tree tries to be a stork
I'm off to Santiago.
When the banana tree wants to be a jellyfish
I'm going to Santiago.
I'm off to Santiago
With Blondie Fonseca
And with Romeo and Juliet's rose.
Paper sea and silver coins
I'm off to Santiago.
O Cuba. O the beat of the dried seeds.
By a hot waist and a drop of timber
I'm off to Santiago.
By the harp of a living tree
By the crocodile
By the blooming tobacco flower
I'm going to Santiago.
I always said I'd go to Santiago
In my coach of blackwater.
I'm off to Santiago

Wood and whiskey on the wheels
I'm going to Santiago.
My coral in the dark
I'm going to Santiago.
By the sea drowned in the sand
I'm going to Santiago.
O the placid cool of sugarcane
O Cuba! Cuve of a sigh and arc of clay
I'm going to Santiago.

SUICIDE

(Maybe it happened because
you didn't do geometry.)

The lad was falling apart.
It was morning, ten o'clock.

His heart was filling up with cloth
Flowers and broken wings.

He knew that only one word
Was left in his mouth.

And when he took off his gloves
His hands shed soft ash.

He could see a tower from the balcony.
He became the tower and the balcony.

He saw, no doubt, how the clock
Watched him, motionless in its box.

He saw his calm shadow stretched
On the white silk-covered bed.

And the boy, angular, rigid
Shattered the mirror with a hatchet.

As it shattered a vast wave of shadow
Flooded the monstrous guest room.

THE DUMB BOY

The boy is searching for his voice
(The King of the Crickets took it)
The boy is searching
For his voice in a drop of water.

I don't want it to speak with.
I'll make a ring out of it
For my silence to wear
On its little finger.
In a drop of water the child
Kept searching for his voice.

In the distance his captured voice
Is changing into a cricket's clothes.

Turbulence

Mystified Einstein. He said he'd ask
For an explanation when he died
But he wouldn't like to embarrass God.
On the eighteenth of April nineteen fifty-five
A wild-haired man tumbled into Heaven
Wide-eyed, waving a stick of pink chalk.
Hypatia, bored in her martyr's robe
Took note. Well well, said the Pharisees,
Things are hotting up around here. And there.

Afterlife

I'm not sure exactly what I believe about afterlife,
I said cautiously, as you do. Listen, my friend said,
I know exactly what happens. They're all up there
At a big cocktail party in the sky clinking glasses
So get ready. It's better than the alternative, I said.
What alternative? she said. No shroud then.

So what'll we wear? Grab your tiara,
Throw a cat around your shoulders
And go. It sure as hell beats Limbo.

Candide

Even in January the sun
After three days of gales
Turns the day on full blast
With a Clapton guitar riff
Then flicks it off again. If
In the silence we see beyond
February to primroses
We are like Candide,
Crazy about spring.

Subtraction

Take islands, Coney or Inis Mór.
Take ditches, moats, the moot
A cursory few stones, with or without
The fortress families erect
On beaches with deckchairs.

Aran in late summer, small kids
Diving off the pier, a race
To the blue boat anchored out
And laughter among the cousins. This
Looking back will be the death of us.

They say it's all about the taking part.
If it is, all we could give were wings,
Salt crystals on skin, a boat.
There is regret, and celebration
That for a while, we were a part of it.

There are shores, with lone figures
Looking west. The strand
Wiped clean, one wind-scrubbed man
Knotted, lumpen. Facing seaward,
Empty as the moon.

Allow him, hovering, invisible
As a shower of particles, that angel
Not hammered from rag and bone
Desperation but cut from dark matter
That causes light to curve, the slight

Refraction of the human heart –
Not much, but enough to put Einstein's
Theory tearing across the world
A telegram from the other side.
'Lights' it read 'all askew in the heavens.'

All Souls

Normally they sit, or walk backwards
But today they stand, leaning forward
In black and white on the quay, waiting
Like extras of all ages, even the baby.

Normally they take centre stage
In colour, voices muted but otherwise
Live through the fourth wall, but today
They all move to the front as one.

They watch our prayers, candles,
Games of divination. Snap apple.
Perhaps it is the children they are avid for
Not us. We will join them soon enough.

Perhaps they need this one glimpse
A year of the living, whom they miss
And all the candles and masses
An excuse. They comfort us, the dead

While they who are now shapeless
Pass through us, a shower of particles
Barely disturbing our pulse, a still projection.
For this, time wrinkles and flows on.

Perhaps while their names are spoken
They are for a moment indivisible, unbroken.
Next year they will come round again
They ask so little. To be named, not forgotten.

At Cré na Cille

The dead roar through the night
On motorbikes, smoking, cursing
Worse behaved than in life.
Wild with excitement over elections, 1916.
Who has new tombstones, who is eyeing who up.
The dead come howling into the conversation
Wreaking welcome havoc.

They rip up the sky, the air, our dreams
And howl at poets and politicians.
They are spark plugs
Kicking life into dead language.
When they leave us suddenly, crying,
Without return dates or promises
Words turn to slugs. The silence is terrifying.

We turn our faces to the wall
Or search the sky for the silver traces
Their words leave but what we want
Is the sound of distant engines getting louder
The women shaking their long hair
Out of plumed helmets, the buzz,
Our sweet Hell's Angels revving up.

A Lift

I.M. DERMOT HEALY

Tell me, is it all atomized energies
Or do the dead, as Baudelaire says, have bad hours?

The world goes on as wicked as before, or worse
Whatever history says. Because of us

We like to think. I'm not so sure. Remember
The time we said a decade of tunes in the car

To pass the time on the way to Derry, you giving
The first one, no stuttering allowed, me answering.

I'd like one more chat as we cross the border
Four packed in the back, faces solemn for the soldier.

Questions about fiddling styles, the long poem –
You were against it – where I stood on the bodhrán

And always the clouds parted and anything, statues
Soho strippers, homeless boys, a sinking cruise ship

Could appear there, out of nothing, like a flock
Of Maybirds because that's also how life is. Pure magic.